T0208202

ZAHIR
THE MAVERICK

ZAHIR
THE MAVERICK

MAN WHO WAS CALLED FOR HIS SERVICE

Shahzada Yaqoot

ZAHIR THE MAVERICK
MAN WHO WAS CALLED FOR HIS SERVICE

Copyright © 2020 Shahzada Yaqoot.

All rights reserved. No part of this book may be used or reproduced by any means, graphic, electronic, or mechanical, including photocopying, recording, taping or by any information storage retrieval system without the written permission of the author except in the case of brief quotations embodied in critical articles and reviews.

Holy Bible, New International Version®, NIV® Copyright ©1973, 1978, 1984, 2011 by Biblica, Inc.® Used by permission. All rights reserved worldwide.

iUniverse books may be ordered through booksellers or by contacting:

iUniverse
1663 Liberty Drive
Bloomington, IN 47403
www.iuniverse.com
1-800-Authors (1-800-288-4677)

Because of the dynamic nature of the Internet, any web addresses or links contained in this book may have changed since publication and may no longer be valid. The views expressed in this work are solely those of the author and do not necessarily reflect the views of the publisher, and the publisher hereby disclaims any responsibility for them.

Any people depicted in stock imagery provided by Getty Images are models, and such images are being used for illustrative purposes only.
Certain stock imagery © Getty Images.

ISBN: 978-1-5320-9279-4 (sc)
ISBN: 978-1-5320-9280-0 (e)

Print information available on the last page.

iUniverse rev. date: 01/21/2020

PREFACE

As I started to write this biography of my Uncle Zaheer, I wasn't sure as to what all I should include. I had a casual relationship with him until the age of 12. He was always after Zahid (his oldest) and I, forcing us to learn the arithmetic, especially memorizing the tables of 2 through the 12th to recite by heart. There wasn't much contact left between his family and I after they emigrated to the United Kingdom. It was many years later that I came face to face with Uncle Zahir in 1976. I was now 24 and fully of haughtiness. But his kindness and patience with me one day came to fruition and I gave my life to Jesus, or more aptly, he succeeded in bringing me to the lord.

Years later when I was stable in my life, I started visiting him in England. Every time he will implant some seeds of faith and send me back with some nuggets of wisdom and advice. Then there was a another gap in my communication with him when I emigrated to the United States. It was in the late 90s, that he started visiting me in California. He was delighted to see Fahmida (my late wife) and I matured in the Lord and serving Him whole heartedly. From there onwards, our relationship became very close. He kept a close contact on the phone and came back to visit us many times. I was always excited to receive him in California and fellowship with him.

When Fahmida was diagnosed with leukemia, he started praying for her regularly on the phone and assured her and I that God was in control and that He would perform a miracle for her. With prayers and treatment, she was fully healed and celebrated her newly given life by traveling to England to meet and thank Uncle Zahir for his relentless prayers that brought her back from the thresholds of death. He was delighted to see her in person, alive and free of leukemia. She was walking around with a replaced immune system that was established through a stem cell transplant for her. Uncle Zaheer rejoiced and thanked God on see a walking miracle standing next to him in his home.

Since we had not attended his 90th birthday due to Fahmida's illness, it was a promise that we will definitely attend the 95th. Unfortunately, I'll be attending that alone as Fahmida passed away in November of 2018. She got into a drug complication that led to multiple organ failures. But she died free of leukemia. I know she will rejoice as Uncle Zaheer's 95th birthday will be celebrated.

This biography that I have basically written in 15 days is based on my memories and the detailed interview I conducted with Uncle Zahir in September of 2019. I wasn't sure as to what title should I give, but knowing that he always did something different, on his own, independently of human help, prompted me to name him a "Maverick". Hence, the title "Zahir the Maverick".

It is my intent to acknowledge all my Family members who were able to contribute important details of many events spanning the last 100 years. Major Rehmat Masih and Ma, were my Nana and Nani jee. Uncle Zaheer is my Mamoo jee. What I have written is basically a close observation of one family by another. I want to thank my cousins Gladys Massey, Gloria Massey, my nieces Samina De Weaver and Sarah Massey who all live in Netherlands. My cousins Salim, Shaheen and Afrin Dilawar(s) in the US, my cousins Sarwat and Cecil Pervaiz who live in Texas, USA, and my cousins in England Zummurad, Zakir, Zene and Zebedee the four children of Pastor Zahir, and also my cousin Shughfta and her husband Pastor Joseph. I would like to make a mention of my beloved cousin brother and Buddy, Zahid Massey, the oldest son of Pastor Zahir, a highly educated man who became a victim of Dementia. His present state of mind and overall health has forced the family to admit him into a Dementia care facility. Amidst all celebration of his dad's 95th birthday, his normal physical presence will be extremely missed. But he will be vividly visible on every heart and mind with his beautiful charming smile. Last but not least, I want to thank my sister in law Heather Massey who was very kind to edit my manuscript and correct several dates and spellings of the proper names.

It is my hope that my family members will laugh a little bit when reading some of the lines that I have purposely written in our native language of Punjabi. An interpretation was written where applicable. A digital copy of this book will also be available for a download later. So if you don't find a time to read it...please listen to it.

Regards.
Chaz Yaqoot. Aka. Kinoo

INTRODUCTION

I am so delighted to see that Chaz has employed time and efforts in writing a biography for our Chacha Jee (our paternal uncle). It was about time to pen down the precious events of his life in the Lord's service. I feel so privileged for spending a quite some time of my life in a very close fellowship with him and our late Chachi Zainab. There are hundreds of memories that so readily come to my mind that each reminds me of their unconditional love, prayers and blessings for me. Chacha Jee has been an inspiration to my life in many different ways. The love he has given me is immeasurable, but the spiritual teachings and in-depth knowledge of God he has so patiently imparted into me is priceless. He has been my spiritual counselor, my teacher, the source of my strength and my confidant with whom I can always share my innermost feelings. Always knowing that he will advise me by his wisdom, and by the guidance of the Holy Spirit. Sister Gladys, joins me here in wishing you all the health and happiness at your 95th. We are looking forward to many more years of your spiritual covering over us to continue basking in the blessings of your love and prayers. Happy Birthday to you.

Gloria Shaheen
Neatherlands.

Dad, thank you for making the decision to come to this country and all the hard work of you and Mum to provide for a good life for us as we grew up. Thank you being an example to us of what it means to love God and serve him wholeheartedly without compromise, for showing us the reality of the spiritual realm, and that because of the total and absolute authority of Jesus, we never need to be afraid. Thank you for being a man of integrity and faithfulness.

Thank you for your love for us and our girls-for praying for us over so many years and for your generosity to us. We would like to take this opportunity to tell you that we love you very much and we thank God for you, all our love.

-Zeb and Heather and family XXXX.

My earliest memories of my dad are in Lahore where all my family lived near each other. I have very fond memories of playing in the sunshine all day and spending time with my Dad who I thought the world of. I remember being very upset in 1963 when he came to England. There was a tree where I used to go everyday to think about him and cry. Looking back now, it was so brave of my Dad to come over here to try and start a better life for us. I owe him so much.

In 1964 we came to England and I was so happy to be reunited with my Dad. He was my Hero. I used to love when he would take me and Zahid running in the mornings. He used to work so hard in order to provide everything for us. We had an amazing childhood and I owe the fact that I have such an amazing life now to all his hard work, sacrifice and bravery.

I can't thank my dad enough for all he has done for me and all our family. His constant prayers for us helps us all and blesses our lives.

I am so happy to be celebrating my dad's 95th birthday with him!

Thank you for everything Dad, We all love you so much.

Your Son,
Zam

Happy birthday, Zahir Massey my dad. Praise God, you have reached the age of 95. There's much to thank you for over the years, and I'm sure you will be happy for me to include our mum Zainab [who is now in Heaven]. We do remember and appreciate growing up with love and security from Godly parents. We recognize the God given ministry, you and mum held over the years, including your time as Pastor of the AOG Church in Ombersley road Bedford. We can all agree, even from those early years at Bedford Pentecostal Church, and throughout our lives, we were able to witness countless miracles within the family and the wider community in Bedford, which included salvations, healings and deliverances. Many people will remember and be thankful to you while giving glory to God.

More recent and since your retirement as pastor, we thank God for your continued health, and we can still appreciate the Biblical teachings you share with us all. Its always a pleasure and privilege when we can meet with you.

Thanks for being the master chef of Asian cooking, and teaching us the recipe secrets for those delicious curries you often made. We are still working on those. They seem to be hit or miss in our case.

Finally, thanks for passing on your Godly nature and qualities of life to us, and even passing on your youthful good looks to your children (me included).

Hope you enjoy your special day, and lets do this again in 5 years, God willing for the big 100. Thank God, through Jesus Christ, we have eternal life.

Your son
Zak Massey

Happy Birthday Dad.

Brian, I and our four sons are all so delighted in celebrating your 95th birthday. Looking back in time, I can cherish each day that you and mum spent in raising us up. Thank you for instilling in each of us a Christian Worldview with all its values from our very early childhoods. Especially, the Godly way you taught me are still a lamp unto my feet and I thank the Lord everyday for giving me a father like you.

Thank you for making sure that our every heart's desire, no matter how big or small was always fulfilled. Thank you for the love and special attention that you gave me as your only daughter. Now that I am a mother and a grand mother myself, I can easily fathom what it takes to raise a family, Thank you for doing this for us so steadfastly and with a big smile always. It made us see Jesus in your persona.

As the only sister of my four brothers, I hereby represent our oldest brother Zahid Massey in wishing you a very happy birthday. And though he was unable to attend in person due to his health issues, we know he is delighted knowing that you have just run past your 95th milestone of life...now jogging towards the finish line of somewhere beyond hundred. May God give you many more years to celebrate. Amen.

With Love
Zene, Brian and the kids.

CHAPTER 1

Zahir the Maverick

Zahir Massey was born on the 8th of February 1925. His parents Major Rehmat Masih and his wife Prem Bai were the Salvation Army pastors of their little town of Dhariwal, a town known for its agricultural crops in Punjab, India. He was the youngest of his 5 siblings. Major Rehmat, who was a well-built man of 6 feet height, would dress up sharply in his grey and red uniform; that was always adorned with ribbons, stars, and medals of merits earned through his years in service. He would compliment his attire with a white starched turban that was skillfully wrapped around the golden dome. Riding upon his saddled black horse he appeared as a powerful man of respect and authority. At that time, the inhabitants of the village that were a big mix of Hindus, Sikhs, Muslims and Christians, lived homogeneously despite their religious differences. Everyday as Major Rehmat's horse gracefully galloped past those people, they would withdraw from his path and robotically raise their hands to touch their foreheads. It was a traditional gesture that signified their reverential submission and a salute to his authority. Major Rehmat loved every bit of it and accepted the given respect with a stiff neck nods with his bearded face that he turned from side to side with split second pauses at various angles.

In those days of English rule over India it was common that people would get arrested for minor infractions and punished under the zero tolerance policies of civic administration. Such policies though based in expediency for the English, were also a necessity to control the rowdy masses of India mostly devoid of civic sense. Now and then even the simpletons of the town will get arrested resulting from their innocent little mistakes. Major Rehmat Masih, who was bold and outspoken, didn't mind calling a spade a spade when needed. Though the English government had established very strict rules and regulations in their governing system, Major Rehmat will boldly appear at the local police stations to rescue those poor people of his village. His service was simply a compassionate gesture for all who genuinely deserved it. Since Major Rehmat spoke decent English, he would confidently sit before the English officers to reason out as to why a certain person was arrested. He would then convince the English officers to free the person under clemency. He was always successful in getting them freed by being bold and outspoken and by exploiting his rank's clout of a Salvation Army's major.

Life was quite simple back then. Need being the mother of all inventions; people were forced to invent their own little things. While the English imported high quality gadgets for their use, the local villagers would notice the benefits from afar and would often create knockout products that somewhat served the same utility. Therefore, when Zahir was born, a single piece of cloth was taken to create a little hammock. The four corners of the rectangular cloth were run through the wooden cot's tightening ropes, and knotted at two ends of the wooden cross bar on the foot-side. The improvised hammock would then be used for baby Zahir to sleep while the mother would engage in the daily chores of her life. That was the initial bassinet or the crib for Zahir. Every time he cried for attention, one of the older siblings would come and give it a push to make it swing back and forth. It cannot be fathomed that was it the motion, or the sudden shock of being violently swung that made the infants quiet, but it worked every time.

Such was the environment as Zahir gained awareness. He was definitely an apple of his mother "Ma". It was pronounced nasally as "Maaan" which was a derivative of the Urdu word "Amma" meaning

2

a "mother". She was not only a Ma to her 6 children but also to the children of her congregation and other village families. Being in a privileged position as officers of the Salvation Army, they were respected and regularly showered with gifts of grains, pulses, lentils, fresh fruits, vegetables and other staples that the villagers brought to them. These were the love offerings by the villagers to their pastors in recognition of their relentless service and unconditional love for all.

The early life of Zahir started by attending a local school in Dhariwal. From the very beginning he was quite serious in acquiring education. Time swept by fast and he emerged as a handsome young man who was done with his high school. All through his senior years at the high school, he had loved math and science subjects, and by now had taken a keen liking for engineering as a subject. The planes flying over his village would often fascinate and inspire him to envision himself becoming an aeronautical engineer. But the resources available to him as one among the 5 other children were limited, and he knew well, that the lengthy route to a six years college program was not viable for him. It was perhaps this realization that motivated him to join the Pakistan Air Force as an apprentice ground engineer. He was envisaging that perhaps one day he will carve out a way for himself to become an aeronautical engineer by first learning hands on training of the jet engines.

In laying a foundation for Pastor Zahir's biography, it will be fair to introduce his five other siblings too. His oldest brother Mubarrik joined the armed forces in a civilian capacity and became a storekeeper. He got married to Mariam and had three sons and two daughters. His second oldest Brother Dilawar, a peaceful man who became a professional stenographer held important posts in various academic institutions of Lahore, Pakistan. He married Sosan and had 5 sons and 3 daughters. Zahir's third brother Gulzar was an adventurous and a daring soul. He joined the Royal Indian Army and for a while was posted overseas to fight in the British Royal Indian forces. He had 3 sons and two daughters. Zahir's two sisters were Mercy who got married to Sunny James and had 1 daughter and 3 sons. The second sister Daisy was married to Mehr Din. They had one son and a daughter.

Pastor Zahir with his 4 siblings.
Left to right are, Mubarrik Massey, Dilawar Massey, Mercy James, Gulzar Massey and Pastor Zahir Massey. This photograph was taken in Lahore in early 1980.

CHAPTER 2

Love at First Sight

When Zahir was ready for marrying, His older brother Gulzar took him to a village name Clarkabad to visit a family whose daughter Zainab was thought as a possible match for Zahir. The custom of the time was to seat the guests in the girl's living room. The prospective bride would then walk in with a tea tray and politely place it on the center table. She would only make a polite time wish to the guests and slowly walk backwards to exit the room. This was considered enough for the man to take a good look on the girl, hear voice, notice her gait, and give either a nod of approval, or just stay quiet and motionless to imply disapproval. So that day after Zanib had made her polite appearance, brother Gulzar looked into Zahir's eyes and gave a quick upward jerk of his eyebrows…a gesture to inquire "so what do you say"? Zahir just smiled and nodded his head up and down about thrice which was a gestured "yes". Brother Gulzar then took the matter up a notch by giving another nod to the girl's father, confirming that the boy liked Zainab. The atmosphere that was a little tense up to now suddenly became euphoric. Zainab's father now had an enhanced reverence for the guests and a gaze of endearment for Zahir. He immediately gave a love token, a currency note of 5-rupees placed on the open palms of Zahir. Now brother Gulzar had to reciprocate. He took out a currency note of 10 rupees and asked the father to invite the daughter back. She returned shying and stopped in the middle of the room; trying hard to restrain her smile.

With her head covered and eyes lowered to gaze at the floor she stood there motionless. Brother Gulzar got up holding the 10-rupee bill and encircling it three times over Zainab's head placed it on her open palms. He then placed his hand on her head and blessed her with few Punjabi sentences that were typically meant for the occasion "Jioundi rae tee-ay" (Live long my daughter). That was all for a full agreement and settlement. Zainab gripping on to her gift money bowed her head and while blushing, turned around to go into the inner quarters. But before going out of sight into the inner house, she stopped, looked back at Zahir and gave him a big smile. Zahir whose gaze was already fixated on her, reciprocated with a smile and a nod. He liked her and was surely in love with her from that moment onwards. In the following days the wedding date was fixed and the ceremony performed and he brought Zainab back to his hometown. Together they started their married life in Peshawar, in the North West frontier Province of Pakistan where Zahir was working at the Pakistan Air Force base.

One may inquire as to why such an elaborate account of Zahir's engagement is mentioned here? Well it is to explain to our present generation as to how God's plan of a man and woman's union in marriage was orchestrated. Ephesian 5.31 For we are members of His body. "For this reason man will leave his father and mother and be united to his wife, and the two will become one flesh." People were driven by this scripture. Firstly, they believed that the relationships were made in the Heavens. And that for every man & woman there was already a helpmate predestined by God. They believed that God would create a situation where there paths will cross and they would take a liking for one another and become one as husband and wife in the presence of God. The union was not a mere experimentation but rather a lifetime commitment to one another based on unconditional love and respect for one another. They accepted one another's likes and dislikes, their respective appearances, moods, habits and their whole beings. The man marrying a woman knew that it was once and for all and that no matter how tough the times may become, or whatever the temptations may come later, he would stand firm like a rock and would not move. The woman in accepting a man as a husband knew that this would be the one and only with whom she will spend the rest of her life. She knew that she would give her heart, soul and spirit in being there for him in all circumstances and that nothing in the world would ever change her mind to think otherwise. She would then commit her self in being a loving wife, a good mother and a stewardess of her husband's household, which for her will be her kingdom. She would protect that kingdom against the wiles of the enemy and would give her life for the honor, respect and welfare of her husband and children.

Sounds bizarre? It does when compared to the societal norms of today. However the norms back in the olden times where different. A simple nod of acceptance was a contract etched in stone. Wordings of the marriage vows that are recited even today, "Until death do us apart", were not merely uttered but rather lived to the fullest.

The present generation may question, what if there were rough edges in the union and that the two individuals were incompatible? Well, the families made sure that the two people being joined in marriage were compatible. Firstly marriage in the Asian cultures was seen as a union of two families and not merely of two individuals. Their due diligence included the family backgrounds, social status, academic levels, financial strength, life styles and propriety as displayed by various members on both side of the families. Once compatibility on such aspects was established, they would then verify physical aspects of age, appearance and specific beauty etc. And if the man liked his future bride and she like him, then the proposal would be solidified and a matrimonial ceremony would come to fruition.

Such were the cultural norms when Zahir got married to Zainab. As it would be read later, the simple nod of acceptance that he instantly gave for his wife, stayed as a contract etched in stone until the last breath of Zainab. We will read more details about their life long journey later in this biography.

Photograph of Zahir and Zainab Massey at
their Dudley street house in Bedford.

CHAPTER 3

Horrific Incident at the Air-Force Base

As mentioned earlier, Zahir had joined the Pakistan Air Force as a stepping-stone to further his career. His initial plan was to get his foot in the door, and then work his way up to become an aeronautical engineer, or qualify to become a commissioned Air-force officer. With this in mind he started learning everything about the mechanics of the fighter jet planes. For a while he was complacent in having permanent job, and having a house given by the Airforce that which his loving wife kept so well. In 1954, God blessed them with a son and they named him Zahid. He felt that him being Zahir, and married to Zainab, was a sign by providence that his linage would all be initialed as "Z". Hence, in naming their first son as "Zahid" they started their lineage that would all have names starting with the letter Z. Their 2nd son was born in 1956 and they named him "Zamurrad".

It must have been around 1956/57 that Zahir had to see a horrific incident at his work. A certain ground technician was working somewhere in the front end of the plane. Another technician in the cockpit needed to start the engine for a test. Once the turbines came to a full spin, an intense field of vacuum was created in front of the turbine. Somehow the person working on the ground walked right into that turbine's vacuum field. In a split second he was sucked up like a fly into the turbine and was minced into a heap of blood and human flesh. By the time the turbine was stopped, there was no trace of a human being but shattered fragments of human flesh splashed within the cowls of the mighty turbine that now stood quiet and lifeless. The gigantic machine that had just swallowed up a human stood emotionless with no remorse or sorrow. It was just a machine that had no conscience or emotions.

The catastrophe left deep emotional scars on Zahir and perhaps that was the day that he gave up his long yearning of becoming an aeronautical engineer. It wasn't long after the incident that Zahir resigned, packed up and returned to Lahore to seek solace and support of his brothers.

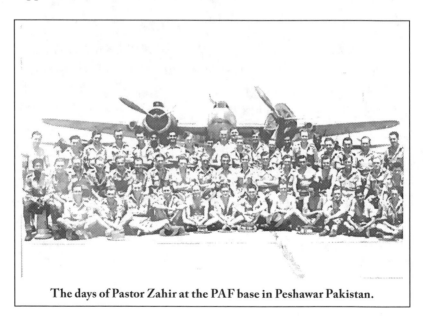

The days of Pastor Zahir at the PAF base in Peshawar Pakistan.

CHAPTER 4

A Bizarre Incident
Witnessed by Zahir

Before proceeding further. A flashback into the life of Zahir deserves a mention. Hence, presented for the readers. This happened on the day Zahir and brother Gulzar were returning to their hometown after finalizing Zahir' marriage proposal with Zainab. As they came out of the "Mian Mir" railway station and had hardly crossed the railway line to pick up the trail leading to Nai Abadi, Gulzar suddenly slipped and fell face down on the ground. Zahir was alarmed as to why he would suddenly slip. He tried to talk to him but he would not respond. Concerned at the situation Zahir struggled to somehow get him up, and with quite some difficulty he managed to make him limp back home. Brother Gulzar still didn't say a word, he was stupefied. Once they were home, Gulzar retired to the bed and Zahir too went into the adjacent home to rest. Next morning he went back to check on brother Gulzar and was surprised to see him sitting alone vacantly staring into the space. Zahir did his regular time wish but there was no response from Gulzar. Zahir now became apprehensive and asked him firmly what was going on and that why wasn't he speaking? Gulzar looked at him with a helpless and agonized gaze with tears rolling down his cheeks. Wiping those away with the back of his hand he gestured Zahir to get him something to write with. Zahir ran and got him a pencil and a randomly placed brown paper bag and hurriedly placed it before his brother. With a little contemplation, Gulzar jotted down a sentence in Urdu and turned the paper bag towards Zahir. It read, "Tang se khanch ker girah diya", the Urdu script he wrote meant "He pulled my leg to trip me". Zahir was confused, wondering what on earth was brother Gulzar talking about? His rationale mind raced to conclude that there was no one except them, so who would have tripped brother Gulzar? He looked once again in Gulzar's eyes and found even more pain and agony there. He was trying to say something but was unable to verbalize. In despair, Zahir ran back to his father Major Rehmat Masih who was sitting puffing his hubble-bubble while reading his favorite book, the king-size bible that he often took out from a wooden case. Zahir quickly briefed him on brother Gulzar's situation and showed him the brown paper bag that Gulzar had scribbled on. Major Rehmat immediately became alert and shouted out the name of Jesus loudly. Then he hurriedly grabbed his turban from his pillow, and after placing it on his head, he tossed it's tassels backwards in a sense of urgency. Holding his "Khundi", (a walking stick with a curved handle), he got up with a super-natural energy and rushed towards Gulzar's house with Zahir in pursuit. They found Gulzar lost in his thoughts and still vacantly staring into the space, and rolling an unstoppable stream of tears down his dark & puffy cheeks. Reaching beside Gulzar, Major Rehmat immediately placed his two wrinkled but still very strong hands firmly on Gulzar's head and shouted, "Get out of my son in the name of Jesus". He then prayed to sanctify Gulzar and freed him from every demonic influence, and pleaded the blood of Jesus on him. While commanding the dirty demonic spirit to let go of their possession on Gulzar, his father blew three times upon his head. As Major Rehmat authoritatively concluded his prayer of deliverance, he opened up his eyes to look into Gulzar's. He then shouted Halleluiah, for he saw that the usual charm and life peculiar of Gulzar, had now returned. Once again, there was peace and comfort on his countenance, and while holding his father's hands in gratitude, he opened up his mouth to praise Jesus himself.

"Shukar ay Khudiya ke toun maree jeeb khol ditee ay, Yesu dey naan de jay, Shukar ay meray Khudiay". He was totally overwhelmed with the deliverance his father had just done through his prayer of authority in the name of Jesus. Brother Gulzar kept repeating the same Punjabi words of gratitude stating "Thank you Lord for opening up my tongue, Praise the name of Jesus, thank you my Lord". He then opened his mouth to inform his father and brother Zahir as to what had transpired the night before. He told them that, as they descended from the railway line and got on to the trail, he spotted a very tiny man sitting defecating on the ground. Seeing that Gulzar explained, he just kicked the little thing on his bare tiny bottom. But right then in a move of self defense, that little creature caught his leg and pulled him down causing him to trip, while vanishing away in the dark thin air. Zahir was speechless, and for a moment Major Rehmat thought lest now Zahir Putar had lost his tongue, but then Zahir spoke out asking, are you sure Pa-jee (brother) that you aren't telling us of a nightmare you had? At this point Major Rehmat who was seriously listening and contemplating while slowly moving his bearded jaw as if masticating broke his silence, "Ho, ho meray bachia, toun Sladey noo dudha mar dita se" (Oh my son, you kicked one of the Cryptids). He then explained that such creatures do exist and though they are small in stature, they have lots of demonic strength and that they are usually invisible to the human beings, but then some human beings had a special faculty of seeing such demonic beings. Apparently, Gulzar Putar (son) had that, but the mistake he made was to kick the cryptid's butt with his boots. For Zahir, the incident left quite an impact but his faith and belief in the mighty power of Jesus was renewed and strengthened, as he knew and witnessed first hand that every knee shall bow and every tongue shall confess that Jesus is Lord. He was convinced that the dirty spirits couldn't stand the very mention of Jesus and thus flee when rebuked in the mighty name of Jesus Christ our Lord and savior.

Picture of brother Gulzar Massey in his late years

CHAPTER 5

Rehmat Masih's Enclave

The parents of Zahir had moved to Lahore from Dhariwal after Major Rehmat's transfer there. By now Major Rehmat Masih was old and starting to frail. His children were all settled in some ways. There were many grand children from all the sons and the two daughters. With the English gone, the prestige of Salvation Army was not the same anymore and it was seen as nothing more than a religious organization that would engage in civic undertakings. They were mostly in evangelizing, and unlike the Catholics or the Adventists and Presbyterian missions, who invested their resources in establishment of educational and health facilities, the Salvation Army did very little. Their few churches were dwindling due to lack of support from the English mission. From there onwards the ranks of the Salvation Army officers lost their glory and became nothing but symbolic. It was in those days that Major Rehmat Masih tripped from his bicycle and injured his head. The injury caused him serious cognitive problems and he was no more able to effectively or logically communicate, or run his affairs independently anymore. All his sons and especially Gulzar decided that it was time for his father to hang up his gloves. Therefore, without much thought or deliberation, Major Rehmat was made to resign from his job. His haste in doing so did cost him a forfeiture of his retirement benefits. He got neither the severance nor any ongoing pension payments. So from being a highly productive man he now became a fully dependent person for his sons. In later years he would realize the mistake made in his hasty resignation from 42 years of service.

By now three houses were build in a row. Gulzar's land was the biggest. He built a house comprising two rooms and a Veranda. Then it was Dilawar's house that sat facing South with three rooms of equal size, a Veranda and a kitchen. Next to it was Mubbarik's house that was just comprised of one extra large room with another longish room built on the East across the bigger room. Another house which was an Indian property left behind was either grabbed or purchased by Gulzar as a second property. That house had just one big room with its outer walls blacked with bitumen and was named Kala Makan. And finally, there was Mercy's home, a big 3-room brick house left behind by a Hindu Doctor.

Major Rehmat Massey who served
the Salvation Army for 42 years
in Ghurdaspur District, India.

CHAPTER 6

Return to Civilian Life

So this is where Zahir returned. He came and occupied two rooms of Dilawar's house. Major Rehmat occupied the third rooms. He lived there alone. His long-term life partner Ma, always shuffled from one home to another living with her sons and her daughter Mercy. It was quite a transition for Zahir to come back to the civilian life. His first concern was to find a job and reestablish himself, and find schooling for his children. With a little effort he did find a job of a works manager at a local automotive company called the Karim Autos. With his mechanical flare he was able to provide car owners service advice and to recommend various maintenance routines on their cars. The most popular cars of that time were the Morris Minor, The Hillman, Vauxhall and Opel Records. There were some Chevrolet Impala, Bellaire and Biscayans. And then there was the Volkswagen Beetle and the Microbus. The smallest car, a Fiat 600, was also there. All in all, there were mostly European cars in the market since the Japanese cars were not yet introduced.

Life for Zahir was stable; it was around Christmas of 1958 that their 3rd child, a daughter was born. She was named Zenobia. Somewhere around this time Zahir landed a nice job in far away town of Joharabad near Sarghoda in Punjab Pakistan. He was there for few years and his 3rd son Zakir was born there in 1962. It was the big sugar mill where he was hired as a service manager. His responsibility was to oversee the fleet of trucks and follow maintenance schedule for each vehicle. This job ended abruptly. Having being appointed there for a while he managed getting jobs for his nephew Gibson Massey and another distant nephew named Karamat Masih. Well at one occasion Karamat was arrested with allegations of stealing a fire pump from one of the truck that came in for service. The police there shut the young man in a cell, hung him upside down and beat him all night to extort a confession that he had stolen the pump and that Zahir was a corroborator. Well, the young guy was innocent but yet took the beating like a real man. He did not agree to false accusations about him or Zahir. After three days of extreme punishment he was let go. Zahir was extremely disturbed at this barbaric treatment of an innocent human being. He thus decided to resign soon and return to Lahore with his family. On his return to Lahore, he intensified his efforts to take an exit to another country where he would find employment and opportunities of advancing himself. The voucher program that allowed citizens of the common wealth countries to gain employment in United Kingdom was an opportunity that he focused on. With his brother Dilawar doing all the administrative correspondence with the British consulate in Lahore, he was soon able to get on the list of candidates. The day came that his sanction to travel came. He was happy to be able to travel and find some employment in the United Kingdom. The family was sad that he had to go that far, especially his mother, who was having fits in knowing that her youngest son would have to travel across the 7 seas to a land far away. He assured her that he would return frequently and that she should be happy that he was given an opportunity to go to Walyat to make a living. Amidst her crying and sobbing she didn't refrain from her last minute advice "Mamain to buch key rawain, tay Zainab no Chathee Chathee sud layain. (Watch out for the British ladies and make sure to call Zainab as soon as possible).

In preparation of his departure, Zahir got a few new woolen suits stitched, got himself a new leather shoe from "Bata", and even asked the local tailor Rahim Buksh to stitch him white dress shirts. He also treated all the young kids to a day out in Lahore Zoo, and on another day to a Movie "The King of Kings" that was a big hit at the box office that winter. Finally his day of departure came. It was a very cold morning of January and the whole family came to Lahore Airport to see him off. Cladded in a new woolen suit and a cap, he was laden with flower and glitter garlands that were heaped up on his chest. Photographs were taken by brother Alfred and amidst a lot of crying and sobbing; he finally walked over to board the plane. Then came back to speak something with his brother Dilawar and then walked back to the embarking steps of the plane. Soon the doors were closed, the engines were fired and the plane taxied off. The whole family kept waving their hands towards the plane. None knew what seat he was on or if he was able to see anyone of them from the plane, but it was a custom that the family had to stand and wave unless the plane taxied away and disappeared behind the trees that separated the runways. That was it, now the family awaited the plane's high-speed dash before a take off. Sometimes it would take as much as 15 minutes for the plane to roar and appear running at high speed. All those present would hold their breath and wait to see the plane take off. On that day of Zahir's departure, once the plane took off, and retracted its landing gears up, it disappeared in the white clouds that were dotted all over against the morning blue sky of Lahore.

CHAPTER 7

Arrival in United Kingdom

Finally landing in London was quite an experience for Zahir. This was the second time in his life that he had touched the British soil. His first visit was an official one when he had to come for training on Bristol Aircrafts that the Pakistan Air Force had bought from England. Before taking the delivery and flying those home, a team of 6 pilots and the technical crew was invited to Bristol England. Zahir was on the technical team and had come to inspect and learn about those planes.

This second arrival in London was different, he had now landed as an immigrant who would be allowed to work and succeed in whatsoever goals he would set for himself. The beauty of the city was incomparable to the place he had left two days ago. People were happy and cheerful; there was law and order in every aspect of life. He truly thanked God for bringing him to England. He had a friend from the Air Force days who had settled in the city of Bedford, England. So he moved over to Bedford to rendezvous with his best buddy Rehmat. Rehmat not only received him with open arms but also took him in as guest in his home. Once again Zahir was overwhelmed with the beauty of the small city and its close-knit culture. It was quite a change from the dirty unpaved roads of Nai Abadi, Lahore from where he left just a few days ago. The cleanliness of the streets, the orderly traffic and parking of the nice cars, the beautifully designed homes that looked all the same at the first sight, but had distinctive nuances when viewed carefully. The color schemes used to enhance the beauty of the English houses with lush green perfectly manicured front yards lined with flowers of all colors at the parameters were all so fascinating for Zahir to behold and admit that God has finally heard his prayers of bringing him to a paradise. At times, he would just smile and pinch himself to check if he was awake and really seeing everything or was it just a beautiful dream? And when convinced that it was a reality, he would be delighted and would start praising God for his mercy and blessings.

Just as every immigrant endures, the initial months of arrival were quite tough. He was still living with his friend from his Airforce times. His wife was quite kind and compassionate. She always made sure that their guest was well taken care of. It took quite an effort for Zahir to find his first job. In the beginning he had high expectations of finding a technical job in his field of aeronautical maintenance. But soon he realized that such jobs required licensing and much higher degree of learning than the one he was trained with in Pakistan. It was hard but he had to convince himself that in order to survive, he will have to hang his suits aside and get into the workers clothing to find whatsoever was readily available. With this resolve he started door knocking at various business enterprises to prospect for a job that would generate a steady income for him.

It wasn't long that Zahir did find a job in a sweets manufacturing plant. Unlike many other people who had come to England from Pakistan, Zahir spoke fluent English so he was given an opportunity to work at a salary of 7 pounds a week. This amount is a pittance in present times, but back in the mid 60s, it was enough to manage expenses of a small family. Everything was priced in Pence and even a 7 pounds seemed like a big amount of money. Being prudent by his very nature, Zahir not only managed his expenses but also started to save every week in preparation of renting a home of his own and to initiate the paper process to bring his wife and children from Pakistan.

His first Christmas in England was an exciting time for him. The holiday vibe that he saw rejoiced his heart. The décor of the neighborhoods, the stores decorated with the beautiful goods available to every common man, and the churches preparing special programs to mark the birth of Jesus were all so beautiful and charming for Zahir to see. He was often overwhelmed with emotions thinking how his wife and children will love those festivities and wished they were there. He then went out and bought some beautiful gifts. A beautiful sweater for his loving wife, two toy pistols for his sons, Zahid and Zummurad, a beautiful doll for Zenobia and a toy car for his youngest son Zakir. He then mailed those out in time to reach Pakistan right before the 25th of December. Finally, it was the summer of 1964 that he was able to bring his wife and 4 children to England. Zainab, with her four Children flew alone to London. At that time their older son Zahid was 10 years of age, second son Zammurad was 8 years, Daughter Zenobia was 6 and Zakir was only 4 years of age. Soon his wife took charge of the household, the kids got into the schools and life became quite busy for Zahir in working long shifts at the sweet factory, managing and overseeing the affairs of the house and coaching his children to advance in the England's school systems. It took them a very short time to get assimilated into the culture and become a part of the English society. Life was more like a machine for Zahir until that time. The salary of seven pound a week now needed to be stretched by being creative. It was hardly enough to make the ends meet. However, his prudent wife Zainab made sure that there was no wastage and that an utmost discipline was practiced in curtailing every expense that seemed an extravaganza. It was doable, and they had a decent life wherein needs of the children were met. They would work 5 days, rest on the weekends and would go to church on Sundays. And in doing so Zahir and his family were content that they were serving God quite all right and that He was happy at their live styles.

In contrast, his older brother Dilawar in Pakistan was on fire for Jesus. He was a devout Pentecostal Christian who believed in a relationship with God and not merely a ritualistic association with Christianity as a religion. He was an elder in his own Church that was headed by Dr. E.J. Sinclair, then principal of Foreman

Christian College (FCC) in Lahore Pakistan. Under the mentorship of Dr. Sinclair, Dilawar had matured himself into the depth of Christianity. His life was a perfect example of Christian discipleship. He believed in the power of prayer and had implemented it in rearing of his own family of 5 sons and 3 daughters. He surely had a burden for others and would always seize opportunities to share the word of God. He was concerned for his own brothers and did his best to bring them to Jesus by his time-to-time ministering. His older brother Mubbarik and his wife Mariam did heed to his advice and became Pentecostals. Gulzar, the younger brother of Dilawar, was a man of his own ideas. And though he practiced Christianity as a protestant Christian, he wasn't really into a close relationship with God in any serious manner. He was more of a philanthropist and believed that giving a big donation to the church was all needed to please God. The third brother Zahir had always been a prodigy of Dilawar, who as an older brother, was delighted in seeing how Zahir would always take his advice to advance himself in life. Zahir too was always very respectful to his brother Dilawar and held him as his mentor in all difficult issues of life.

As Zahir settled in Bedford, England, he kept a constant contact with this brother Dilawar by way of writing him letters. Seeing that Zahir has now settled, brother Dilawar researched for a spirit filled church in Bedford. He was successful in finding a Pentecostal Church in Zahir's town and immediately took an initiative of writing a letter to the Pastor of that Church. Introducing himself as a born again Christian, Dilawar wrote an introduction about his brother Zahir and requested the pastor to initiate a contact, and to bring Zahir and his family into the fold of his church. The pastor of the church was moved on reading such a letter coming from across the oceans, therefore without any delay, he too took an initiative of visiting Zahir's home and invited them to attend his church. Zahir and his wife Zainab were first surprised but knowing that the instruction to visit that church had been initiated by his brother Dilawar, started attending that Church. They were very welcomed there, and were soon implanted strongly into the teaching of Pastor Douglas Quy who was gifted with an anointing in the ministry of healing and demonic deliverance. Zahir and his wife become more and more involved and soon dedicated their lives and committed themselves to the Church of God. It was affiliated with the Assembly of God worldwide ministries. It was 1964 that Zahir gave his life to Jesus and was saved. In 1965 he took water baptism that signified his spiritual rebirth and hence declared 'Born Again' in his relationship with triune God representing Father, son and the Holy Spirit. His wife rejoiced in this spiritual transformation of her husband, she herself had been saved and already water baptized in Pakistan many years back.

CHAPTER 8

Spiritual Growth

Zahir's walk with the lord after the year 1965 took an acceleration. He was fully committed with his heart, soul and spirit to learn the word of God through his discipleship with Pastor Douglas Quy. The growth was slow and gradual, but he left no stone unturned in researching the Christian faith from various angles. After being equipped with the foundational teachings, Zahir continued learning and researching into the depth of God's word. He would peruse the Holy bible closely, annotate it, understand it literally and then strive to draw a spiritual inference. God had given him a sharp and intuitive mind; therefore he would often think outside the box and receive revelations inherent within the lines. In his research he would rely on the hearing the inner voice of the Holy Spirit and not the by-products of his intellect. His prayers were inspired under the unction of the Holy Spirit and not those that are recited from the memory or verbalized from a script. He watched over his body in the physical as well and made sure that enemy had no entry through the eye or ear gates. Therefore, he only watched good and inspiring Christian programs and listened to good Christian music. He loved his native tongue(s) of Urdu and Punjabi, and therefore, enjoyed reading his Urdu bible side by side with his English King James Bible. The more he researched, deeper the knowledge he acquired.

In 1966 Zahir and Zainab were blessed with another son. In line with the names of all other children he was named "Zebedee". They were rejoiced to have a 4th son. The family became known as the "Z" family because of their names that all started with the letter Z. Zahir & Zainab and their five children named as Zahid, Zammurad, Zenobia, Zakir and Zebedee. Both Zainab and Zahir loved their five beautiful healthy children and thanked God for blessing them with such a harvest. As the children became busy in the schools, both Zahir and Zainab became more and more involved in their Church ministry. He was convening weekly worship services for the desi community comprising families from Pakistan, India, Sirilanka and Bangladesh. Pastor Douglas Quy graciously facilitated the meetings and other events of the desi community at the Church of God, premises.

It was in one of the church meeting that a need for praying upon a certain person occurred. To this point in time, he was more of a support to Pastor Douglas Quy and would often stay back to intercede and agree with him in the prayers rendered by him. However, on that particular day, the Spirit of the Lord moved him internally and compelled him to come out of his shell and boldly manifest the anointing that God had already bestowed upon him. There was still a certain hesitation on his part. A doubtful thought kept popping up suggesting that it was not his place and time to move forward and lay hands on the one being prayed. But then the Spirit of God rebuked his internal negative thoughts and gave him confidence by reminding him that he was the co-heir with Jesus and that he too was given an authority to do great and might works in the name of Jesus. He then boldly stepped forward and placed his hands on the person being prayed upon. Pastor Douglas Quy was delighted in seeing the breakthrough that Zahir had just accomplished. Later he commended Zahir for his initiative in laying hands and praying in the spirit for the needs of the oppressed person. Thus that particular event was an inception of Zahir's personal ministry. God then used him mightily within the Indian and Pakistani Christians residing in Bedford and the nearby towns in 50 miles radius. God took him overseas as well to proclaim the word of God. As he got busy with the works of God his faith grew and he learned depending upon God's provision rather than the rewards of his own physical work. Then he had a health setback. He was diagnosed with a heart disease and was recommended an open heart Surgery. Doubt and fear again came to his mind. He was fearful of the surgery and doubtful of its success. Negative thoughts occurred day and nights and persuaded him to cancel the surgery and just give up. He then reckoned the tricks of the enemy that were manifesting in form of negative thoughts in him. With this realization, he took charge over his own thinking pattern and rebuked the negative thoughts out of his mind and sanctified himself with the blood of Jesus. He was at peace and felt confident in boldly going in for the surgery. He knew that God Himself would manifest through the skillful hands of the surgeons to whom He gives wisdom, knowledge and expertise to correct what had corroded within the human system. He realized that it is not God who sends us the ailments but the tricks of the enemy that causes us to neglect our physical care that results in form of health problems. His surgery was a quadruple bypass. It was a success and doctors congratulated him by announcing that they were granting a 10 years life extension to him. Zahir smiled, for he knew that he will be believing in the report of the Lord and that God is the giver and taker of lives and that it is up to Him to number the days of his life. We'll touch upon this subject later but in brief please know that this is the 32nd-year beyond the heart surgery. After recovering from the surgery, Zahir went back into the affairs of his ministry. He was busy praying for his community needs collectively as well as individually. Many strange and miraculous events happened during his fifty years of ministry. Somewhere simple but some were quite complex. The readers of today may find it incredible that the bad spirits and demons play their tricks on people of God. But bible proves the presence of such beings. Ephesian 6 describes how the devil has established a rank and order in his dark kingdom. But in the Indian and Pakistani community of Bedford and its nearby towns the influence of the evil spirit seemed running rampant. And though, Pastor Zahir dealt with hundreds of such cases, we will mention a few that seem to be quite strange and thought provoking.

The next chapter records some of the miracles that God did through the hands of Pastor Zahir.

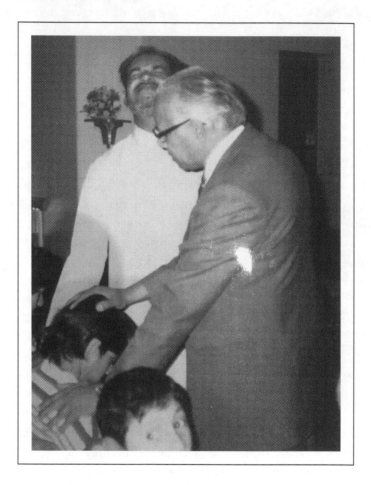

CHAPTER 9

The Miracles

The First Miracle

Zahir flourished quite rapidly in his spirituality under the mentorship of Pastor Douglas Quy. When he got saved in 1964, he was totally on fire for Jesus. He would attend several church meetings every week and seize every opportunity to grow spiritually. Slowly but gradually he started to mature in his gifts. The gifts of the spirit started to manifest in and through him. He would pray for others, lay hands and would rebuke the devil for oppressing various people at his church and community. A day came that he had to visit their community Tailor's house where his wife Zainab wanted to pick-up her clothes. While conversing, the tailor asked if Zahir would be kind enough to drop him to the community Jeweler's house. Zahir agreed since he too knew that person well. On getting there, the Jeweler informed that they were going through a very tough time with their daughter. When Zahir inquired further, they informed that she was possessed with a demonic spirit. Zahir being bold in the lord asked the jeweler, the girl's father, if he would allow Zahir to speak to the girl directly. When Zahir addressed the girl she clearly spoke back in a hoarse male voice stating that he was the demonic spirit of girl's grandfather and had taken spiritual possession of her. Zahir immediately discerned that he had to cast the demonic spirit out of the Hindu girl. Knowing that the family was of Hindu faith and that they had their Idols all around, Zahir sought the permission of her father to pray in the might name of Jesus. He boldly told them he had no respect of reverence for any their idols and that when he would pray he would call upon the name of Jesus. Pastor Zahir sanctified himself spiritually by seeking the help of Holy Spirit. Then took authority by calling upon the mighty name of Jesus and the covering of His blood. He boldly and authoritatively rebuked the demonic spirit. And when he laid his hands upon her, the anointing from his hand touched her and that very moment she was freed from the stronghold of the demonic spirit. Her countenance changed and she was immediately transformed from an aggressive and agitated person possessing a foul mouth, to a quiet and calm young lady. Upon whom the God had just been merciful. Pastor Zahir raised his hands to thank the miracle working God who had anointed him to cast out a demon in the name of Jesus and by the power of his blood. Pastor Zahir then advised the Jeweler to maintain an atmosphere of Christian praise and worship in his home and to wean out his home from the collection of his idol gods.

The Second Miracle

The first miracle at the hands of Pastor Zahir was the inception of his healing and deliverance ministry. His hometown Bedford and the surrounding small towns were populated with many Indian and Pakistani families. He soon started to hold meetings for people of the sub-continent India, Pakistan & Siri-Lanka etc. The Punjabi Sikh community was large. Sikhism is an offshoot of Hinduism with some adopted variations. Pastor Zahir was always bold in sharing the word of God with all Desi people. He would invite them to his church. People liked his polite nature therefore readily agreed to visit his church. His second miracle was in the Sikh community. He states that a certain married woman was ill with a chronic issue of blood. She was brought to Pastor Zahir with a request for a prayer for her illness. When Zahir politely inquired her name, the woman spoke back in a hoarse male voice and informed that he was the residing spirit of a serpent that is usually the size of a python. Pastor Zahir rebuked the demonic spirit with full authority declaring. "I command you in the name of Jesus to leave the woman alone and never ever return to possess her again". The power of the Holy Spirit, gave strength and utterance to Pastor Zahir to continually rebuke the demonic spirit that was impersonating as a "python" to get out of her in Jesus name. Finally the girl was freed from the stronghold of the demon. She was transformed once again as a kind and loving woman who later accepted Jesus and became a witnessing Christian who attended Pastor Zahir's church for a long time.

The Third Miracle.

An Anglo-Indian person from India came to Bedford. He claimed to be an itinerant preacher who had come to England to spread the word of God. Pastor Zahir compassionately took him to home as a guest. He stayed there for a week during which he would go along with Pastor Zahir to church activities, and then return home with him too. There was one strange routine that this visiting preacher had. While returning home, he would often insist on being dropped off at the embankment some distance away from home. Pastor Zahir thought it was just for exercising so didn't pay much attention. Since he had stayed with Pastor Zahir for a week already, another Pastor Ghulam requested Pastor Zahir, to allow him to host the itinerant preacher at his home. Pastor Zahir agreed. The itinerant preacher packed up his luggage and waited for Pastor Ghulam' s arrival. But in the interim decided on going out on his walking routine. Looking at his packed belongings, pastor Zahir got a strange thought of opening and searching one of the handbags. Pastor Zahir wasn't sure as to how he should proceed. His morals and propriety prohibited him to look into another person's belonging, yet the spirit within him was compelling him to take a bold step and search the closed hand bag. Finally the spirit of boldness came and compelled Zahir to search the hand bag. With mixed feelings of boldness and hesitation, he opened the hand bag and was shocked to see cigarettes in his baggage. It was a very big surprise for Pastor Zahir to discover a good amount of cigarettes in the hand bag of person who was proclaiming Jesus. Now it dawned on Pastor Zahir as to why the man always wanted to get off on the embankment and would go out on walking routines. He was seeking privacy to smoke and satisfy his addiction. Pastor Ghulam did pick the man up and took him home. Pastor Zahir felt obligated to inform Pastor Ghulam of his finding cigarettes in man's hand bag. So Pastor Zahir and Pastor Ghulam agreed to search further in his baggage whenever an opportunity allowed. It was just a day latter that Pastor Ghulam was able to thoroughly search into the hand bag and was astonished to find pornographic materials. He immediately informed pastor Zahir of his finding and they both decided to confront the man that particular evening. The man argued and came up with several lame excuses of having cigarettes and pornographic materials with him. Pastor Zahir asked him to leave Bedford immediately. The guy then became rude and confrontational and questioned pastor Zahir's authority of asking him to leave. Both Pastor(s) Zahir and Ghulam were firm to him and therefore checked him by paying a one-night charge at a local hotel for him.

Pastor Zahir recalls this incident and attributes it to the awakening of the Holy Spirit in him. In the natural a polite and humble person like him will never do such a bold thing as opening a guest's hand bag. However, that particular evening, the Holy Spirit quickened him to do so. Pastor Zahir's residence was always kept sanctified by continuous praise, worship and the prayers. In such a spiritually sterile environment, the presence of addictive materials had no place. The man who was clearly a hypocrite had brought that sinful pollution into Pastor Zahir's house. This was unacceptable to the Holy Spirit and He was the one who quickened Pastor Zahir with a thought and then with an action to reveal a sinful situation. The degree of the sinful situation was intense and therefore the holy spirit wanted that to be cleared out soonest possible since Sin and

Holy Spirit cannot coexist. Therefore, the Spirit gave boldness to Pastor Zahir and latter to Pastor Ghulam to face the devil head-on and to cast the darkness of sin out from the habitations of Holy Spirit. The awakening of the spirit in pastor Zahir is definitely a miracle. Miracles can only be done under the unction of the Holy Spirit. However, the Holy Spirit cannot and will not allow sin to co-exist. To this day pastor Zahir describes this miracle of revelation with a lot of enthusiasm and is humbled by the very experience of being led by the Holy Spirit to do something that was socially inappropriate. But he defines the experience as a clear learning message from God. He explains, that though we have a free will and a choice to conform ourselves to social norms but when God inspires you to take a certain action, one must set all worldly norms and social etiquette aside and follow directions of God. A lot of discernment is also necessary in taking actions against the devil. The word of God warns us to avoid carnal (physical) confrontation with the devil. In the physical realm, he is definitely stronger but he is weak and crippled when confronted in the spiritual realm. (Cite) The weapons of our warfare are not carnal but spiritual in Jesus name.

The 4ᵗʰ miracle.

Zebedee had an African American friend named Kirk who was in the lord. They would often pray and worship together. The gentleman was surely on fire for Jesus. One eve Zebedee came in rushing to his father Pastor Zahir, informing him that there was something seriously wrong with his American friend Kirk. He said he was just behaving wild and obnoxious. Pastor Zahir immediately sensed in his spirit that his son's friend was under a demonic attack. Rushing along Zebedee, they found Kirk not only behaving weird but also grunting like a pig. His changed countenance, his manifesting aggression and his voice that was emulating a real pig was all so strange and eerie. Without wasting even a minute, Pastor Zahir immediately called upon the Holy Spirit for his assistance. Taking a full authority in the name of Jesus he bold and loudly commanded the tormenting spirit possessing Kirk, to leave in the name of Jesus. As Kirk paused, Pastor Zahir rushed in to lay hands over Kirk and spoke the prayer of deliverance upon him, rebuking again the demonic spirit to leave Kirk. Pastor Zahir continued to command the stubborn spirit rebuking it in the might name of Jesus and declaring that the virtuous blood of Jesus was shed for Kirk to be freed from all oppression, therefore, leave in the name of Jesus. Immediately, Kirk fell in Zebedee's arm like a leaf of a tree. His countenance changed to normal, he stopped all agitation, his voice became as his original and he started to praise the name of Jesus once again. There was such an atmosphere of joy at this marvelous miracle that God used Pastor Zahir. It was a miracle of deliverance. The cunning Satan who reigns in his wicked kingdom on this earth often plays his direct tricks by oppressing those that are serving God. He hates those who are obedient to the tenets of God. He torments them by his dirty tricks and often takes an entry into some lives when they become spiritually vulnerable. But nothing can stand before the name of Jesus. Jesus casted out dirty spirits from a man, and casted them into a herd of swine who once possessed then jumped off the cliff into the sea. Thus destroying all the dirty spirits into the depth of the sea.

Pastor Zahir' continued for many more years in serving his community with his ministry of deliverance. In the process there were many disciples who benefited from his in-depth teachings of the word of God. His humbleness and simple nature were his biggest assets. He was totally oblivious of all the worldly things. He always believed that God would make all kind of provisions for him. He was always very content with his life and in fact, he was benevolent towards others. He was full of empathy and thus could not bear hardship or misery of others. His very nature being calm and compassionate was often misconstrued by the secular world. There were instances where some other Christians whom he had helped establish themselves in England, would end up misbehaving in arrogance and would insinuate him. One such incident he experienced was with a certain Indian man who had come to him a while back. And even after he had settled and established himself in Bedford area, his mail was still being addressed to Pastor Zahir's address. On receiving a letter in his name, Pastor Zahir presumed it as important and therefore decided on delivery it to him in person. As Pastor Zahir brought him a letter addressed to his name, the man behaved totally as a jerk. Instead of thanking him for delivering his letter, he turned around and verbalized an obscene remark. Pastor Zahir was taken aback at such an unwarranted remark and did not understand as to why someone who was being done a favor would respond so diabolically to his goodness. He was offended in the natural and for an instance thought of smacking that man hard for being an outright jerk, but then the next moment the spirituality in him overcame the carnality of his being. At that moment, he apologized to the man and moved on. He latter prayed for the man to have God's peace to come over him. Pastor Zahir analyzed the whole scenario and discerned that the man was probably going through deep depression resulting from his personal problems. The way he had reacted the Pastor Zahir was not fair and had no justification whatsoever. Pastor Zahir then prayed for him and when he recited his daily Lords prayer, and got to the closing sentence that "Forgive our trespasses, as we forgive those who trespass against us", the few simple words of the Lords prayer became so live, he realized that he was not just expressing those words verbatim, he was actually living it. It was such a feeling of joy, peace and contentment that came over Pastor Zahir that his eyes became wet and some tear drops rolled off his check to slip on to his lips, instinctively he licked and tasted the salty fluid that was so soothing to his soul. His prayer in simple English then transformed into the heavenly language of prayers. The unction of the Holy Spirit was so strong that he cried like a little baby and babbled in the spirit. Having lived the very words of the lord that day was so immensely comforting and contending that he just stayed there in a praying posture until engulfed in a peaceful sleep with the holy blanket of God's love and grace.

The 5ᵗʰ Miracle

Having travelled to India and Pakistan a few years back, he had made several new disciples in those two countries. With a revolution of the Internet around the world, came the facility of calling internationally for a very low cost. This was something big for People of Pakistan who would often pick up the phone and call Pastor Zahir. Sometimes, even at the very odd hours of the night. People calling him from those countries just did not have the sense to respect the time difference. They did not realize that when they working, Pastor Zahir was sleeping. Yet, he will wake up and attend to their calls. One such person was a tailor by the name of Alam. Having been disciple by Pastor Zahir during his visit to Pakistan, Alam would often go to far-flung villages of Punjab Pakistan to evangelize and to hold meetings to teach the word of God to the simpletons of those villages. Alam then asked Pastor Zahir for a financial help to launch a tailoring business in Lahore Pakistan. Pastor Zahir advanced him a sizeable amount of money to start a tailoring shop in one of the prominent markets of Lahore. Though he took a start, but he did not study the competition that existed for him. There were other Muslim tailors who did not like the idea of a Christian coming into their territory to start a high end tailoring shop. He was first verbally threatened, and when he did not budge to their threats, the orchestrated a grand theft into his shop. Alam had also complained earlier of another problem for him. He apparently was suffering from a sense of confusion. Any material cut to make a certain garment went wrong, in the middle of the job he would realize that he had cut the material wrong. In desperation, he called Pastor Zahir to inform of his situation. On listening his ordeal, Past Zahir immediately discerned the spirit of confusion oppressing upon that man. Pastor Zahir asked the man to use the speakerphone while he was going to pray. Pastor Zahir sensed though the telephone call that there was heavy witchcraft influence on that man and his shop. Telephone was the only contact available for Pastor Zahir to pray. He recalled the scripture that "We will send the word and the word

36

will be effective", the man was prayed upon in the spirit, his shop was spiritually sanctified by the blood of the lamb and at that time, God gave a discernment to Pastor Zahir who advised the man to shift his shop to another town where there were many more Christians living. The man did change his business address, and soon thrived there. To this day, he is thankful to Pastor Zahir for his council and spiritual guidance.

CHAPTER 10

Five Decades of Ministry

There are scores of other Miracles that Pastor Zahir has performed with the power of the Holy Spirit. In his ministry spanning over 5 decades, he was used by God to bring hope and healing to those who were oppressed. He being a family man always made sure that his priorities were set right. He raised his five children in a Godly manner. The oldest son became a very successful mathematics teacher who taught at the high school level. The other three sons went into the construction industry where they succeeded in various aspects of the trade, his only daughter married a wonderful man and together they have raised a family of 4 sons. Pastor Zahir has a total of (11) grandchildren and now also has several great grandchildren. He is a man full of love; therefore, all his children adore and respect him.

It was around 1990 that his beloved wife was diagnosed with Alzheimer. Pastor Zahir became her primary caretaker. There were lots of challenges in conducting activities of daily living. But he being a man of God knew that it was his responsibility to take care of his wife to the last day of her life. It was over Ten years of extreme difficulties before she was finally admitted to the nursing home. Her condition had become worse and reluctantly Pastor Zahir had to agree on sending her away. She passed away after being a short time in that institution. It was a quiet a devastating setback for him. Loneliness was the major concern. He was otherwise pretty independent in his routines but there were times he would long for a companion that he could talk to, someone who could empathize with him and be partner in his ministry. God made it possible for him to remarry a very noble lady who was sincere and loving to him. Together they travelled to other parts of Europe and twice to the United States.

The writer of this biography is Pastor Zahir's nephew who resides in California. Allow me to write in first person tone in describing some of my early life interactions with pastor Zahir. Pastor Zahir and I had quite a rocky start in the mid 70s. Pastor Zahir was visiting Pakistan for the second time and was evangelizing all over Punjab. It was 1976, I had just returned from New York unsuccessful in settling there. He was quick in asking me as to how was my relationship with Jesus and that if I had given my life to him. Obviously, I was not a churchgoer, and other than a symbolic attendance at the church on Christmas every year, I didn't know much about God and Jesus. As he started quoting scriptures in support of his spiel, asking me to give my life to Jesus. I had million questions for him. My argument was against the religion as I attributed everything to Science. Being an avid follower of Carl Sagan who presented "Cosmos", a program that explored the universe and its million of stars and planets, I was almost like an atheist. However, Pastor Zahir listened very patiently and did not get annoyed, rather kept smiling and giving me more scriptures to back up his case for Jesus. There were more than three such occasions that we sat down to discuss but every time we will just end up without me giving up. I later left for Kuwait to work and got busy, but then somewhere in between I came to visit Lahore and met my uncle Pastor Zahir again. We had a very pleasant time together. We flew to Rawalpindi together to go meet my sister there. I was just missing going back to Murree hills, so I seized that opportunity to first drive up to Murree with Uncle Zahir and then return to Rawalpindi to see my sister. Later we caught a flight back to Lahore the same evening. That meeting left quite an impact on me. I saw that though I was always haughty, uncle Zahir was always calm. And though I had a never-ending array of agnostic questions, he always came back with a rebuttal based on a scripture. His peace, joy, steadfast love, patience and forgiveness towards my arrogant arguments made me realize that he was driven with many superior values than the one I was. On my return to Lahore, I pondered further and deeper and realized that how God's hand was operative in my life, how God had blessed me with good work and every blessing of the world. In a very short time of about 2 years after my arrival in Kuwait, I was quite established with a little business and a family. I was already married to Fahmida by that time and had our first Child Sonanina.

It was in the drawing room of my cousin Ikhlaq, that I finally gave my life to Jesus. Uncle Zahir led me into a short prayer of salvation and declared that I was now saved and that from there onwards, must spend my life in serving Jesus in whatsoever way I could. That was the beginning of my journey with Jesus. However, the change in me was slow and gradual. Kuwait being a Muslim country didn't have many churches. There were little fellow-ships that were formed by various Christian leaders from Pakistan where I visited a few times with Fahmida, but I did not connect there at all.

It was the summer of 1982 when one day I got a call from Uncle Zahir informing that he was in Kuwait and that the immigration was not allowing him an entry. I was pleasantly surprised but at the same time didn't know how to get him in. In desperation, I called Fahmida and informed her of the situation. She said she'd see what could be done. Within 30 minutes she called me back and informed that she was able to get a 24-hour visa for him and that she was going home with him. I was delighted to know that he was given and entry. I rushed home and met Uncle Zahir, who informed that the immigration had asked him to go to the immigration office next morning to get an extension for his visit visa. Well the next day I tried my best to get him an extension but the bureaucracy of the Kuwaiti immigration was such that would give a run around from one office to another. Uncle Zahir who was use to the British ways of handling things gave up on getting an extension and since there was still a time left for the British Airways flight to London, asked me to just take him to the Airport. That's what we did, picking up his luggage from my home, we rushed to the airport in time where he took a flight back to England. In between my running, I managed to take a couple of photo shots for him.

It was few years latter that I met him again in London. By now we had two children. Mami Zainab was alive and she took such a good care of us during that Easter weekend. Sister Gladys and her two daughters were visiting from Holland and together we all had a wonderful time in Bedford and London. This wasn't my first visit to Bedford. I have been there before during my business operation with Fleming Pederson in Luxembourg. I would travel to Luxembourg every 2nd month and on my return will stop in London. From Heathrow I would take trains first to Kings Cross station and then to Bedford. I would stay a day or two with Uncle Zahir before returning to Kuwait. I remember, in one of my trips, Uncle Zahir took me to his work place. Those days he used to work at a snooker club in the busy downtown of Bedford. At the work-place I say that there were several snooker tables where people came and rented for specific number of games. There were some slot machines too where people will spin to win cash prizes. I was quite curious as to how Mamu Zahir felt working at a place where the slot machines were used? He explained that he was just the operator of the place and was not the owner or collaborator of that business. His involvement in the business was of an active employee who was following the policy and procedures of the business owner. My question was based upon my notion about the slot machines. The concept of slot machine is rooted in gambling. People are tempted to insert their coins in hope of winning big money. Its one in a thousand chance that the machine may give out some money, rest it keeps in its reservoir. The process is a sophisticated swindling of people's money by a mechanical swindler. And so, I wondered how a pious person seeing all this, would tolerate people losing their hard-earned monies. Uncle Zahir spoke to me at length on this subject and convinced me that his involvement was that of an arm's length. He was just an operator and not a corroborator of the business that offered the gambling opportunities to people. He also informed me that he would often seek openings to council young players who would frequent his place every weekend. And that there were many who listened to his advice and in fact gave up their habit of playing slot machines. Uncle Zahir worked there for several years. Since he was an honest and hard-working employee, he was retained for a long time. It was later in the years when his ministry flourished that he had to say good-bye to his employment there.

CHAPTER 11

Zahir's Life in Nutshell

There were many more miracles done in his ministerial time. It would take a lot of time to reiterate every one of those in detail. Pastor Zahir was active on all days of the week in visiting people who needed his prayers. He was an anointed teacher of the word. People reckoned his Christian World View and admired the moral values that he exhibited. His persona was seen as the true manifestation of the fruit of the spirits as defined in the bible, "But the fruit of the Spirit is love, joy, peace, forbearance, kindness, goodness, faithfulness, [23] gentleness and self-control. Against such things there is no law" Galatians 5:22-23 New International Version (NIV). People found him full of love that he showered not only upon the people he knew but even to the total strangers or anyone who ever came to him. He was always joyful. He never became nervous or scared or apprehensive about any circumstances of his life. He lived a nice peaceful and happy life with his pious wife and 5 children. The portion of blessings he received from the Lord always fulfilled him. People say that he was always content and never had avarice or any otherworldly desires. People always found him at peace. All his life he newer had a quarrel or any disagreement with anyone that could lead to a confrontation. He emulated peace, as Jesus had ascribed. No worldly worry was bigger than his Jesus who had promised that no matter how difficult the situation, one's peace should not compromise. Pastor Zahir was stable minded all through his life.

Reason being that on facing a challenge, he would analyze it by his critical thinking and come up with a solution that was always inspired by God who had given him wisdom to discern and then decide under His inspiration. He was also an epitome of forbearance. He was able to absorb a whole lot of challenges, setbacks, challenges and pressures of the world, He did so by relying on the mercies of God and His promises that He will never leave or forsake those who are obedient to him. Pastor Zahir's kindness, goodness and faithfulness has been incomparable in many areas of his life. Such as taking people in to his own home to help them get established, going out of his way to lend money to others in need even when they were thousands of miles away. And responding to others needs in a swift and positive way. And when it came to gentleness and self-control, his life speaks for itself. His gentleness at times has even been construed as his weakness but he has always emulated the gentleness and self-control as taught by Jesus. He never jumps to conclusions and is always calculated in his approach in responding to others. There were times that he was insinuated by people whom he tried to minister or bring them to Jesus. But with his gentleness and self-control Pastor Zahir through his God given wisdom, defused the situation and even turned it around to normalcy.

People thus loved learning the word of God from him. They saw Jesus manifesting through his behavior and God inspired teachings. He was expository teacher who would provide a rhetorical analysis under the unction of the Holy Spirit. When he taught them the word of God from Bible, he would not rely upon his own thoughts or understanding but would wait to hear from the Holy Spirit to inspire him in expounding on the given scripture. He taught his people to hear the voice of God within them and become sensitive to His commands for their lives. He taught them about the gifts of the spirit as defined in the bible "But the manifestation of the Spirit is given to one for the profit of all: for to one is given the word of wisdom through the Spirit, to another the word of knowledge through the same Spirit, to another faith by the same Spirit, to another gifts of healings by the same Spirit, to another the working of miracles, to another prophecy, to another discerning of spirits, to another different kinds of tongues, to another the interpretation of tongues. But one and the same Spirit works all these things, distributing to each one individually as He wills." (1st Corinthian 12:7-11). And just as God had bestowed the gift of "working of miracles" for him, he encouraged others to seek God in identifying their respective gifts of the Spirit. He always emphasized that it was in recognizing one's gift that becomes a working miracle in their lives. Many gifts of the Spirit were identified in his congregants who once aware of their newly found gifts unleashed that to promote the kingdom of God and the rule and reign of Jesus.

It was 1980 when Pastor Zahir's oldest son Zahid Massey decided to get married. Since it was the first wedding of the family, both Pastor Zahir and his wife were overwhelmed with joy and started planning it in a big way. As arrangements were made, invitations were sent overseas to ask all the guests to attend the wedding. Though there were many relatives already residing in Europe, Pastor Zahir sent special invitations to his 3 brothers. His two older brothers Mubarrik and Dilawar Massey(s) were still in Pakistan while the 3rd brother Gulzar Massey resided in Kuwait. Finally they were all able to come and attend the wedding. It was after quite some time that the 4 brothers met. It was quite a family reunion as people from all over Europe flocked in at Bedford to participate Zahid's wedding to Janet. There were memorable photographs taken of the family that still adorns the family albums of many family members. It was such an atmosphere of love and unity as the four brothers came together and once the wedding festivities ended, they all got together to reminisce their childhoods, to talk about their father Major Rehmat Masih, the life in India, their decision to settle down in Lahore, the building of the houses, their children being raised together in big compounds and enjoying unity and love that was enriched into their very upbringing. The recalled the many mini-wars they had with other inhabitants of the colony. How, they were able to dominate the area despite being surrounded with Muslim homes. In nutshell, they replayed their respective lives spent in Pakistan and how they had raised their families and with so many young men who were all well built and daring. The days of their visit in London were limited but they caught up with one another's lives and then parted again with a heavy heart leaving behind the memories that would then be cherished through the photographs till this day.

The Ministry of Pastor Zahir continued all through the 90s decade. By now God had blessed him with a lots of respect in his local community. People adored him for his humbleness and faithfulness in serving the Lord. His children were all married and well settled in their lives. Seeing them all take their respective places in the society gave pastor Zahir a lot of contentment. He and his wife Zainab would often reminisce all the hard work they had to put in raising a family of five children. They would often praise and worship God and then lift up their hands to thank Him for his mercy and love. They would always acknowledge how God's hand had been operative in their lives and that how God had come through for them so miraculously and taken them out of financial difficulties and other challenges of life. With the children settled, they now had some discretionary finances available that they would use in travelling. There were several members of the immediate family that were spread all over the globe. There were hardly any people left in Pakistan, they had all taken an exit and had settled in Belgium, England, Holland, France and the United States. His brother Dilawar had settled in Bristol Connecticut in the US. Whose oldest daughter Surriya was the pioneer to come to States and get settled. For Pastor Zahir, his brother Dilawar was a personal mentor and a source of spiritual inspiration. It was in the early 90s that Pastor Zahir took a trip to Connecticut accompanied by his youngest son Zebedee. This was his first visit to the United States. He was delighted to see the good life of his brother Dilawar. Pastor Zahir had a wonderful time with his brother and mentor. They discussed the word of God at length and shared their experiences with one another of their respective lives in the service of Jesus.

The five successful children of Pastor Zahir. Clockwise,
they are Zeb, Zahid, Zak, Zam and Zene.

CHAPTER 12

Challenges with Zainab's Health

The decade of the 90s started well. By now his second son Zamurrad (Zam) got married, as well as his only daughter Zenobia (Zene). His third son Zakir preferred being a bachelor and that's the way he lives to this day. Youngest son Zebedee (Zeb) was still at home but had just started dating a young lady Heather whom he wedded in 1991. It was around 1994 that Pastor Zahir wife Zainab started to show signs of mental disorder. She started forgetting things. Within few years her dementia took toll on her ability to remember anything or to think cognitively. It was quite a challenge for Pastor Zahir to cope with her rapidly growing symptoms that in the beginning were simple and charming, but soon started to become problematic. Though she was able to perform most of the household chores, she just wasn't able to systematically engage her mind in anything that she did. She was able to make "Chapaties" (Pakistani tortillas), but instead of retaining them in the holding box, she would just toss it into the trash bin. She just didn't know what she was doing, and perhaps in her perception she was even being productive. Pastor Zahir became her primary caregiver. He would make sure that she was safe at home and that she would not end up doing something that could hurt her. For this reason, he would never leave her alone. When going out to shop, he will just take her with him. At one instance, he took her to a super market to shop groceries. There Zainab ended up hijacking some other lady's cart full with her groceries. When the woman asked her cart back, she adamantly told that the cart was hers (Zainab's) and that all the groceries were hers. The other woman being wise, just backed off and smiled away, perhaps comprehending Zainab' state of mind. Pastor Zahir than gave Zainab a diversion and was able to bring her home. Another time she was able to sneak out several books from the bookstore. Next day Pastor Zahir took the books back to the store and explained them the situation. A time came Zainab declined totally and was unable to carry on her activities of daily living. Pastor Zahir still stood steadfastly by her and never became angry or frustrated. As a man of God he endured every hardship and fulfilled his responsibility to the utmost. Then finally, he had to make the harsh decision of checking his wife into a skilled nursing home. It wasn't an easy decision but he prayed about it and God spoke to him convincing him to hearken to His voice that clearly gave him the message that it was in Zainab' best interest that she should be admitted to the Nursing home. Zahir finally felt a little relief and was able to review his personal and ministerial assignments. Eventually, Zainab passed away. Pastor Zahir was devastated but as a man of God he knew that his beloved wife was mortal and had gone home to her creator to live in eternity.

Life became a sort of lonely for Pastor Zahir. However, he diverted his energies to study the word of God even more. It was some time later that God brought another person in his life. She was a widow who was known to Pastor Zahir and his family for quite some time. A marriage proposal was made and they solemnized their relationship in a simple wedding ceremony. Pastor Zahir's household was once again established with a helpmate. Daisy was and still is a wonderful lady who serves God alongside her husband. Together they have a great companionship. Twice, they were able to travel together to the United States. Pastor Zahir's family became fond of her and held her in high esteem. Daisy being a pleasant person always left a positive impression on the hearts of people she met. She is a great cook too. Every time she came to California to visit my family, she was requested to make several traditional dishes of Pakistan. God had given her a prowess in culinary. They make a great couple together and are able to laugh together at each other's jokes. Pastor Zahir celebrated his 80th birthday with his second wife Daisy in the year of 2005.

Then it was time for Pastor Zahir to hang his gloves from the active pastoring of a church. His health and old age were one factor. Being a pastor is a special call and requires a lot of dedication and energy in shepherding his flock. No matter how big or small a congregation of a Pastor be it is still a full time commitment that needs to be fulfilled no matter what. The congregants who attend a specific worship place at will often gravitate towards a church because of its location, or the richness of the spoken word, the anointing that manifests from the specific pulpit, the enthusiasm of the praise and worship teams or simple the Charisma that the Pastor displays. All these elements were present in the church that was led by Pastor Zahir; however, the physical age and wellness were of the concern. The energy required to shoulder this responsibility was on a downward spiral. In view of all this Pastor Zahir decided to delegate his responsibilities to Pastor Joseph Barkat, He was the nephew-in-law of Pastor Zahir and was well trained and educated in the word of God. Pastor Joseph took over the reins of ministry and fulfilled its responsibilities in a manner that was quite all right. Gradually, Pastor Zahir took an exit from an active role as a head Pastor to that of a figurehead. Later, he totally withdrew himself from all responsibilities of the church and became secluded in his home. However, he would still pray and minister to the people who would always reach him to seek comfort and guidance at their difficult times.

CHAPTER 13

Heather "The Angel"

It was 2016 that the four sons of Pastor Zahir determined that it was not safe for him to stay alone at his residence. It was decided that he would move in with his youngest son Zebedee. Who being in the construction industry, remodeled his home to create another bedroom for his dad. Pastor Zahir has lived there for the last 3 and a half year now. As mentioned earlier, Zebedee got married to a beautiful lady Heather, whom God brought into his life at the Kings house Church in Bedford. Zebedee married Heather in 1997 and they had two beautiful daughters Megan and Amy. The daughters had grown up by the time their grandpa Pastor Zahir came to live with them. Zeb's wife, Heather is a very smart, caring and hard working housewife. The care and concern that she renders to her father in-Law Pastor Zahir is amazing. She is so disciplined in her routines that she won't delay even a minute in doing what was scheduled. Her typical day starts by fixing breakfast for Zeb before he leaves for work, then for Amy and exactly at 8.00 AM she lovingly serves a breakfast for Pastor Zahir. Usually a big array of breads and various spreads are placed on the table for him to make a pick. He often takes cereal with some toppings that Heather makes it for him at exactly 8.00AM and is usually done in about half an hour, before moving to his sitting room in front of the house. There he has his books, a computer with a printer and other publications of his interest. He is quite adept at the computer and puts it to a good

51

use by maintaining his presence on the social media and researching Google for spiritual articles of interest. In updating his face book, posting his comments on various threads and communicating with emails are all a part of his daily routine. These activities provides him with good mental stimulation that is conducive to his retaining a great memory. It is amazing to note that despite being so well seasoned, he can still recall and quote bible scriptures with a perfect relevancy.

At exactly 10.00 AM he gets a soft knock on the door, It is Heather's way of seeking his permission to come into the room, to deliver a cup of tea and biscuits. That is Pastor Zahir's 10.00 AM snacks that Heathers brings it in on the dot. Then around noon, Heather returns to his room with a list of some written numbers. She would sit and inquire as to what meal number would he like for that particular day. Pastor Zahir, who has memorized all the numbers would deliberate for a moment and then resolutely informs- "Today I'll take number 752, dear". Hearth will then check the stock availability to confirm availability and if available it would be served in 15 minutes. Its amazing how Heather gets involved with the nuances of his diet and makes sure that he is given what his heart desires. Evening tea is then served at 4.30 PM followed by his dinner at 7.00 PM. After that he rests in his room for an hour before retiring for the night. Heather also makes sure that he is taking his medicines at time, and that his clothes are dropped or picked up from the dry cleaners. Heather does all this with love and patience. She is always pleasant and manifests the agape love that is so richly imbibed in her. Seeing all what Heather does for her Father in Law, only makes us believe that God has appointed an Angel in-charge over Pastor Zahir. Thank you Heather.

CHAPTER 14

Life in the Retrospect

Pastor Zahir's present life evolves around reading, listening to his collection of Urdu worship songs, watching a little bit of TV and being active on the social media. He maintains a page on Facebook and checks for messages and status updates of his 200 plus Facebook friends. He holds regular telephonic bible studies with family members in Europe. Every Tuesday at 4.00 PM, he holds a telephonic bible study with his niece Gloria Shaheen who lives in Netherlands. He has systematically taught and trained her in the teachings of the bible. Through these teachings she has learned to handle difficult situations of everyday life in a confident and fearless manner. She thanks him for investing his time, energy and sharing such a vast and rich reservoir of spiritual knowledge so patiently with her thus giving a spiritual growth for her. He longs to travel again but due to weak health and restrictions imposed by his doctors he is avoiding it. While reminiscing his humble beginning in Dhariwal, India to his present day life of opulence in England, he can't help thinking of the hard work, struggle and the sacrifice his wife and him had to employ for the happiness and upbringing of his children. He remembers how he bought his first home on Dudley Street and the sheer happiness that it brought to his wife at the ownership of her house. How the five kids grew up and took their respective places in the society. Sometimes he drifts back to reminisces about the ministry of his own Dad Major Rehmat Masih. He recalls how even then, Christianity was under persecution from the Hindu and Muslim fanatics. He holds a certain event in his memory that he heard so often from his mom and dad as a faith building tool for him. It was many years before his birth, that Major Rehmat Masih's home was surrounded by some radicals who wanted to burn him, his wife and their first born child Mubbarik, alive by setting fire to the hay bales around his home. They were many and were fierce in their anger and fury. Major Rehmat who would usually stand up to such aggressors realized that he was seriously outnumbered and therefore decided to fight the attackers spiritually rather than physically. He gathered his family in one room with his wife, and knelt down to pray asking God to act on his behalf and cause the mobsters to back off and spare him and his family's life. As Major Rehmat prayed, the angry mob tried to set the hay bales on fire, but were taken aback as the apparently dry hay that was highly combustible, did not catch fire. After continuous efforts when the mob did not succeed lightening up the fire, they retreated in frustration, as they were unable to comprehend as to why the hay will not ignite. With the mob gone and out of sight, major Rehmat thanked God for his divine help in saving him, his wife and child. He realized that God's ways were definitely higher than his. He knows the future and that particular day he knew that at some particular time the mob was going to attack his house. But that very morning heavy rain, showered and soaked the hay bales with water making those incombustible. God had pre-planned a rescue for Major Rehmat and his family. He had brought the intime rain, for he knew how the devil would attack Rehmat Masih's home through the angry mob, he knew how they would attack him and use the hay bales to harm him, thus rendered the weapon of their warfare useless. It was a faith building experience for the Rehmat and his wife. In later years, they would often share it with their children to build up their faith and confidence in the mercy of God for his people. Ma, would often gather her children on her bed every night and would tell them to cuddle up with her in her quilt. Once she had all gathered around her, she will tell them various happenings of life as her version of the bedtime stories. Though a simple women, she understood well that the more word of God she would pour into her children's ear, longer it would stay and guide them through the difficult time of their future lives. Such was the foundation for Pastor Zahir. Trust and dependence upon God was imbibed into his upbringing, he grew up believing that no matter what the circumstances dictate, his God will always come through for him. He often recalls his service in the Pakistan Air force, where many employees were fanatics. It was a time right after the partitioning of India and formation of Pakistan. The newly formed Pakistan had no resources and needed to reestablish its defense arrangements. Zahir would work alongside fanatic Muslims who had just played the games of bloodshed with the migrant Hindus and Sikhs. The bigotry was still running rampant with uncontrollable emotions that caused people to go irrational at trifles. Many a time the Muslim colleagues would insinuate Zahir for his Christian faith, and many would like to pick a verbal or even a physical fight. But Zahir would always use his wisdom and defuse the situation tactfully.

An earlier incident in India had left an impact on his life. There was a certain fanatic who hated Sikhs. At a certain occasion this man somehow got hold of the keys to the armory from where he stole several rifles and a stockpile of ammunition. He then enticed some Sikhs to come into his work place. As soon as the Sikhs came into his close range, he started to shoot at them randomly and took them down. His religious bigotry totally impaired his inhibitions and he did not realize even for a minute that what he was doing was a barbaric act of violence against some innocent people whose only fault was that they were not of the fanatic's faith. These incidents left some deep scars on Zahir's heart. He would often think as to how he could bring a change, how he could do something to rid people of their prejudices and bigotry. Being rational he would only reach one conclusion that he could not fight these people in the physical but can only pray to God to change their hearts and bring a change in them. Later in the years, these were the reasons that he started contemplating an exit from the Pakistan Air Force. By now he had realized that no matter how hard he would work, the chances of him getting commissioned were slim and though he could continue as a service engineer, he would never be able to succeed as per his expectations. It took him well over 2 years to finally make up his mind to resign from his permanent job with the Pakistan Air Force and become a civilian once more. By then he had two sons, Zahid who was about 5 and Zamurrad about 3 years younger to his brother.

Presently, Pastor Zahir though physically frail has an outstanding cognition. His long-term as well as the short-term memories are excellent. He can instantly recall all the happenings of the past nine decades as well as the current affairs of his life. He attributes this to God's grace and mercy upon his life, and his strict discipline in activities of daily living, including the quality and quantity of the food intake. One will never see him nibbling on any kind of junk food, desserts or snacks. He eats qualitatively in small portions that are good to sustain his physical strength and energy. This discipline was self instituted many years back when he had to undergo an open-heart surgery, a quadruple by-pass with doctors assuring that another 10 years were added to his life by the wonders of the medical science. Well that was some 30 years ago. Once out of the surgery, he gave himself a resolve that he will never eat any fatty or sugary foods. He fixed his portions and intake timings for his three meals a day along with adequate exercise routines and refrain from indulging in eating more than necessary. The holistic approach of nourishing his body with good food intake, nourishing his spirit by reading and absorbing the word of God and harnessing his psychological health by maintain positive thoughts are all conducive to his present longevity and well being. The life time bible research that he undertook as a young man in 1964 is still continued, and even though he has perused bible all his life, he still finds it very fascinating to read a scripture and receive a brand new interpretation from the Lord. He explains that Bible is read spiritually and not merely physically. Any verse that is casually read has no impact except its literal meaning. But when a verse is closely read and pondered upon critically, it brings a new revelation and a new meaning or a fresh inference. The receiver relates this to personal anointing and one's closeness to God and draws inferences and finds ways of implementing those in personal life or lives of others.

Pastor Zahir enjoying his 10.00 AM tea and snack time.

CHAPTER 15

95 years Young Now

Pastor Zahir has now turned 95 years of age. Even at this age, he is filled with the joy of the Lord and lives a life full of positive energy. When asked how long would he like to live, he smiles and says, "I am hoping for a rapture". His sense of humor is still intact and he never misses a beat in sharing a quick witty remark when appropriate. His 95th birthday was planned almost 5 year ago when he turned 90. That birthday was celebrated with a lot of pomp and show. Relatives from all over Europe and the United States flew in to give him a one big surprise. At his entry when he saw so many people waiting for him, he was overwhelmed with emotions. He realized how much he was loved and that how his love for all was being so aptly reciprocated with reverence for him. The evening was full of fun and a resolve was made then and there that God willing his 95th birthday will be celebrated likewise. At the 95th, there will be even more people coming from all over Europe and the United States. We know that he will be blessed not only with lots of love, prayers and well wishes but numerous tangible gifts as well. It is quite a challenge for one to find an appropriate gift for a fulfilled man of God like Pastor Zahir. For one, he is not into material things at all. Being blessed beyond measures he lacks nothing and there is nothing that he longs for. Secondly he would rather like to see something of a benevolence done, rather than an expenditure incurred in tangible gifts many of which may be redundant for him.

One of the gift that was planned for him is this brief biography that was written to record his life story. It was his desire that his immediate family and friends know the details of his humble beginning in India. He wanted to share a little bit about his parents, and their life style in British India, his siblings and how they all grew up to take various routes to establish themselves. Many were struggling all through their lives and few were just complacent in their mediocre lives. The two sisters Mercy and Daisy were a little unfortunate. Daisy and Mehr Din died at a very young age leaving behind their two children Isabella and Dhul (his real name is not remembered) who also died before the age of 12. Isabella, was raised by her maternal uncle Gulzar. Mercy and Sunny James had 4 children, the daughter got married at a very early age and left the folds. Of their two sons David and George, the later died at the age of 10. Then after some twelve years of gap another son was born. They named him Joseph James, but then when he was only two years of age, Sunny James died in a road accident. Mercy became a widow when she was only 35 years of age.

Pastor Zahir also wanted his children, grand children and several great grandchildren to know of his academic yearnings, occupational endeavors and quest for getting ahead in life. He hated being complacent in life and always wanted to strive for his family's advancement. Had he not been so, he would have stayed settled in Pakistan and continued a mediocre life of survival. That would have definitely impacted his children and generations that were to follow. He wanted to remind his family as to where he came from and how he ended up in England and made it a home. But most importantly he wanted to share his spiritual transformation. He wanted to remind them of his conversion from an ordinary Christian to a highly active servant of God. He wanted to tell his children, grand children and great grandchildren about hundreds of people who came into his life in the 5 decades of his service to the Lord, and as to how each one left a certain impact on him that helped him mature and succeed in the service of God. He wants to teach them the many benefits of hearing directly from God and obeying with a blind faith in his promises. As he did all his life, even when the circumstances were difficult, he steadfastly moved forward in his service to the Lord. Last but not least, he wanted to leave a written history of his life for his children and grand children and great grandchildren to read and retain as to how dramatically God works in our lives, and even when we try to take it easy or even ignore him, he never does to us. In fact, he is concerned about our welfare and long-term futures. He even orchestrates events that we do not comprehend in real time but only realize those in retrospect. With these emotions in mind this biography was put together. It is not a book intended for public viewing but rather a very private history of a man who had always listened to the voice of God and acted upon it.

The few stories of his miraculous healing service are just a glimpse of hundreds similar that were performed during the span of his service to the Lord. His intent in narrating these events was never to self-exalt but to glorify God who used him as a conduit to manifest his mighty miracle working powers. Pastor Zahir never thought of himself anything other than being a God's vessel that was full to meet the needs of others only. The humble life of simplicity led by Pastor Zahir symbolized Christ and his teaching. His contentment in serving the Lord was such that he was and still is oblivious to all worldly attractions and charms. So much so that the common entertainments like TV shows, or secular movies or even visiting to the theme parks in Europe and America were never on his agenda. His biggest delight was to visit churches, meet the pastors, attend their services, meet the people and then introduce himself by keeping a low profile. Many pastors would then recognize his contrite spirit and anointing that flows along one's refined conversation and propriety, would often compel Pastors to ask him to preach and lay hands on the people who needed deliverance through the power of prayers. Pastor Zahir would welcome such opportunities and would pray and seek God in picking a subject to minister upon. Many a time people will acknowledge at the end of church services, that the substance of his sermon blessed them and that God spoke to them and gave them clarity of mind after listening a specific message from Pastor Zahir.

There is a little regret noted in the narratives of Pastor Zahir. He often states that his response to God's calling was a little delayed. He concedes that he should have taken up the ministerial work much earlier in life. He thinks the time he has spent in the ministry could have been much longer had he come into God's service a little earlier. He feels so knowing that his brother Dilawar, who was a true and committed servant of God, had tried all his life to activate Zahir into the service of God. His brother Dilawar was a born again, spirit filled and tongue talking Christian who was always concerned about various members of the family. He loved his younger brother Zahir the most among his siblings, hence always focused on Zahir to bring him into God's folds the earliest. Zahir on other hand was so engrossed in concerns of life that he never seriously thought about his brother Dilawar's propositions. Instead he continued relying on his own abilities and trying his best to make a living for his family. He was progress minded and strived one way or the other in finding a breakthrough for himself that would eventually change the financial status of his growing family. God gave him an idea and an initiative of actually researching possibilities of taking an exit from Pakistan and settling somewhere in the Western hemisphere where the social system was at parity and that one's ability and ingenuity was recognized. He thought of settling in England and that's where he finally came and settled. In this process of establishing himself, he was fully focused on his work that brought him a steady income. Obviously, Zahir at that time did not know the power of living by faith and asking God for every provision. He depended more on his own abilities to produce for sustenance. Brother Dilawar on the other hand was man who lived by faith and knew well that it was not his concern to worry about his needs, but rather believed on God's promises and to fully believe that whatsoever he would ask in Jesus's name- God will provide. This truth was finally imbibed into Zahir through his discipleship of Pastor Douglas Quy. Pastor Quy was a man who believed in every written word and taught the same to his disciples that when asking from God, one had to trust God and pray ceaselessly and patiently until the breakthrough would come. But once, the transformation came in Pastor Zahir's life, he became an epitome of faith. From there onwards he left all his worries at the feet of Jesus and instead stood by the scripture that if he would first seek the kingdom of God, then everything else shall follow. And that's exactly what he experienced. He was amazed as to the surplus blessings that came to him through the blessings that his children and congregants bestowed upon him. He was never short of finances and in fact he was able to bear the costs of his own evangelistic tours to Pakistan and India. Once there he would bless other Pastors of small churches in various towns of Pakistan. He even helped some poor people to startup some small businesses without requiring them to ever payback the invested finances. Therefore, his financial help was never given as a loan but an outright benevolence.

The reason behind recording these traits is not to exalt the man in any unjustified way but to portray his compassionate nature and Christ like persona. Being kind hearted, he cannot accept someone being in trouble or hardship. He is empathetic towards the needs of others. This is one value that he wants to get perpetuated in his children's and the generations that will follow. He has lived all his life helping family and friends and that's what he would like to become his legacy that should be continued when he finally takes an exit from this world some day. His children understand this and his sons Zam, Zak and Zeb and daughter Zene have jointly assured him of their commitment to continue his legacy of unconditional love and help to those who deserve the most.

POST-SCRIPT

I want to thank every reader who has taken the time to read the pages that I have written in presenting my uncle Zahir Massey's biography. It was my little attempt to touch upon the known aspects of his life. In doing so, I have just touched the tip of an iceberg. I am sure if few others who may decide to write after me on this great man of God will have their own recollection of personal memories with him. His four sons and the daughter, nieces and nephews, children in-law(s), and the community members who had the first hand experience of seeing, meeting and worshiping with him may have many more of his values and virtues hidden within their hearts. I encourage them to please step forward and share those treasures with the family to add more substance to his biography. Maybe they can write on his very personal habits or about the things he liked the most in others. They can perhaps write on his threshold of emotions. What made him worried, what caused him to snap, what made him laugh and was anything that would make him nervous? I ask this knowing that there is still a lot to be discovered in the personality of Pastor Zahir. This biographical narrative for him was based on my relationship, distant observations, and the two days of intensive interviews that I conducted with him in September of last year. I feel, a lot may have been missed out.

The clarity of his statements verbalized mostly on the strength of his memory, in a humble attitude without any efforts of self-exaltation but crediting God, for using him for His service was enough of his ethos for me to authenticate all narrated events. He further substantiated his narrative with numerous recorded video recordings, photographs and written works.

I was really impressed with his very organized thinking pattern. He would use some notes to jog his memory to pickup a cue on which he would then expound without any signs of digression or going on a rabbit trail. His math skill is still intact and he can mentally calculate big numbers for mathematical calculations and even dates of major events or historical happenings. Being an avid reader he has quite an extensive vocabulary and an impressive command of the English language. Even though English was a second language acquired through the early stages of his life, he reads, writes and speaks it with perfect fluency and eloquence. He is never hasty in replying to questions but is deliberate. While talking to him one can see visible signs of comprehension on his brows as he begins to process incoming information. What he hears is processed through the filter of God's word to draw an inference. He would then look at it critically to compose his response. A visible heaving appears on both sides of his temples as he processes, composes and softly delivers a response that is always wise and non-controversial. He is conscious of the fact that words have power and so does the tone that is used to deliver. He believes that even the finest spoken word when delivered in caustic tones can negatively impact the listeners and distort their inference. Therefore, most of the time when he makes a statement, he would also leave a follow-on question to engage the listener and ensure that he or she properly inferred what he had implied.

He has been a peacemaker too. In his ministry of over 50 years, he not only healed the sick and the oppressed but also reconciled many broken hearts. His Godly counseling has restored numerous marriages. However, he has always supported the truth, just and the innocent. He would evaluate and support the victims against aggressions and mal-treatments. Many among the community that he served often came in with their baggage of malice, jealousy, bigotry and often habits and practices rooted in their original cultures. Such people never got rid of their cultural mindsets, habits and practices. Misogyny that gives birth to domestic violence was one such practice that Pastor Zahir had to deal with quite often. Male chauvinistic behavior of some men coming from the third world countries often manifested in beating and battering of wives for unprovoked reasons. To make it worse, the submissive attitudes and helplessness of the fearful women who would stay silent, would often encourage husbands to repeat and intensify their daring maltreatments by gross misuse of their earning capacities. Some were simply conceited for being male and thus considered themselves superior in strength and thought it justified to beat and torture their women physically and emotionally. And just as major Rehmat Masih stood up for the simpletons of his village, Pastor Zahir too boldly stood up against such atrocities and aggressions of men. He helped in dissolutions of such meaningless marriages and enabled the victims to take a fresh restart and embark on the path of a new and reformed life by first serving God and his kingdom. In accomplishing these results, Pastor Zahir do not consider these as miracles but reforms accomplished in the physical realms by coming to rescue the numerous helpless souls who would have otherwise perished in their gruesome situations.

I feel my closing thought will not be complete if I do not mention of his physical appearance and lifelong dress code. God had given him good looks. He is more after his father Major Rehmat Massey. With a decent height and proportionate physique, Pastor Zahir was complimented as being handsome young man of sophistication. In fact all Massey brothers loved dressing up sharply for their offices, and especially when attending church services on Sundays. They wore suits, neckties, closed shoes and hats. At home they all dressed up casually in white pajamas and long shirts (kurtas) but never in Dhooties, as it was more popular among the Muslims and Hindus. Major Rehmat Masih taught them the importance of coming before the Lord not only with a pure heart and spirit but also their physical bodies, the temples that God had given to his people for the indwelling of His Holy Spirit. He taught them that the Holy Spirit is conscious of the spiritual as well as of the physical cleanliness. Furthermore, he also taught them, that if we have to dress up so sharp to please our worldly superiors in the offices and institutions, how much more important it is to come before the maker of the universe the Lord God Jehovah. They were taught that coming before the lord in an unclean or messy way would grieve the Holy Spirit, and thus hindered to come in to the presence of the Lord. And though Jesus taught us that it was not only the purity of the physical self but the sanctity of the Spirit that matters the most, it does not warrant us to appear before God indecently or in shabby attires. Therefore, those who have seen Zahir during the last 5 decades will readily agree that he was and still is a sharp dresser. From the very young age, he was very fond of wearing tailored suits. He has kept that interest all through his life and became so habituated that even though he has taken a retirement you will never see him without a jacket. As culture took a little turn, he too has softened down a little by not sticking to the suits but has shifted to blazers and trouser combinations in many shades of navy blue and grey with white shirts. Lately, he is only wearing half sleeve shirts with Sweater or cardigans that are quickly switched to navy blue blazers when going out for appointments or fun. His shoes are always shinning. It is perhaps a habit that originated in the Pakistan Air-force's uniform maintenance routines that he still follows regimentally. During his active preaching years, he would always wear suits, with wing tip or toecap black or brown shoes. His colors were always coordinated; making sure that his socks always matched his trousers. He was never hirsute, thus have been clean-shaven all his life. Seems that may have contributed to his young looking, wrinkle-free very healthy skin that he maintains even at 95. His energy level now has deteriorated and though he takes light sitting-down exercises, he is hopeful to do more walking and aspires travelling within Europe at least.

We know that he is mortal, and one day God will either rapture him, or take him home in the most pleasant transition from this world to the next. Pastor Zahir boldly talks about this and is not afraid but in fact excited about graduating to the next realm of life. He absolutely knows what waits across the thresholds of this world.

A life eternal where there is no pain, suffering or any other limitation of the body, but rather an ambience of continuous praise and worship by the host of Angels before the throne of God. However, we who will be left behind to feel his physical absence among us are concerned for the last standing fighter of the Rehmat's clan. The last one of his generation who has fulfilled the mission that was once started by a daring and yet very humble village pastor of Dhariwal, Major Rehmat Masih. That last child, the youngest son will some day leave this planet and transforming immediately back to his spiritual form will return to his creator the God Almighty. We are sure, he will be welcomed at the pearly gates where his credentials in God's relentless service would have prequalified. Pastor Zahir will be placed into his promised Heavenly mansion. Would there be our rendezvous again with him? Surely, when we all graduate to his level of spiritual accomplishments, we too will be ushered into our respective Heavenly mansions, some big, some small. But no matter how big or small our rewards in Heaven may be, let us strive to secure it while we have time here on earth. We serve a God of compassion and love and He will be just to us.

Now our prayers are that as long as Pastor Zahir is with us, let us strive together to follow on his footsteps and follow the trail that he has created. Let us all give one another a promise to emulate his life that was so enriched with spiritual and physical blessings of God. Let us love and respect one another for that will be the ultimate fulfillment of my Uncle Zahir mission on Earth. Our hats-off to you sir, for the beautiful fight of faith you have fought and have come out victorious. We all promise that your legacy will perpetuate through your children's children and that your name will always be revered and honored and remembered by the generations to come. Amen.

Printed in the United States
By Bookmasters